TECHNOLOGY TAKES ON NATURE

LEVEES AND SEAWALLS

BY ERIKA EDWARDS

Gareth Stevens PUBLISHING

Please visit our website, www.garethstevens.com. For a free color catalog of all our high-quality books, call toll free 1-800-542-2595 or fax 1-877-542-2596.

Cataloging-in-Publication Data

Names: Edwards, Erika.
Title: Levees and seawalls / Erika Edwards.
Description: New York : Gareth Stevens, 2017. | Series: Technology takes on nature | Includes index.
Identifiers: ISBN 9781482457759 (pbk.) | ISBN 9781482457773 (library bound) | ISBN 9781482457766 (6 pack)
Subjects: LCSH: Levees–Juvenile literature. | Sea-walls.
Classification: LCC TC337.E39 2017 | DDC 627'.42–dc23

First Edition

Published in 2017 by
Gareth Stevens Publishing
111 East 14th Street, Suite 349
New York, NY 10003

Designer: Sarah Liddell
Editor: Ryan Nagelhout

Photo credits: Cover, p. 1 Sherry V Smith/Shutterstock.com; background texture used throughout Matlinkski/Shutterstock.com; p. 5 Brian Nolan/Shutterstock.com; p. 6 Josef Hanus/Shutterstock.com; p. 7 Johnny Lye/Shutterstock.com; p. 8 Andrei Stanescu/Shutterstock.com; p. 9 Francis Dean/Contributor/Corbis Historical/Getty Images; p. 10 Nikodash/Shutterstock.com; p. 11 DanMS/Wikimedia Commons; p. 12-13 Mario Tama/Staff/Getty Images News/Getty Images; p. 14 Anton Watman/Shutterstock.com; p. 15 Stephen Morton/Stringer/Getty Images News/Getty Images; p. 17 Justin Sullivan/Staff/Getty Images News/Getty Images; pp. 18-19 Ashley van Dyck/Shutterstock.com; p. 20 JamesChen/Shutterstock.com; p. 21 Jim Edds/Getty Images; p. 22 Oppdowngalon/Shutterstock.com; p. 23 Upload bot (Rich Smith)/Wikimedia Commons; p. 25 Jorg Hackemann/Shutterstock.com; p. 27 JOSH EDELSON/Stringer/AFP/Getty Images; p. 28 Marilyn475/Wikimedia Commons; p. 29 Armita/Shutterstock.com.

Printed in the United States of America

CPSIA compliance information: Batch #CW17GS: For further information contact Gareth Stevens, New York, New York at 1-800-542-2595.

CONTENTS

Words in the glossary appear in **bold** type the first time they are used in the text.

WHEN THE LEVEE BREAKS

In today's world, we do our best to protect ourselves against nature, but things can still go wrong. In 2005, a large storm called a hurricane hit Gulf states like Louisiana and Mississippi. Hurricane Katrina hit New Orleans, Louisiana, especially hard, weakening the **levees** around Lake Pontchartrain. Some of these levees gave way, flooding the city.

The man-made levees and **seawalls** meant to protect New Orleans often go unnoticed until something goes wrong. Let's see how these structures take on nature and what happens when they fail.

WORSE THAN KATRINA?

The worst river flood in US history was known as the Great Mississippi Flood of 1927. It happened when levees along the Mississippi River broke in 145 places. Rushing water flooded over 26,000 square miles (67,640 sq km), killing at least 246 people and perhaps as many as 1,000, and causing $100 million in **damages**.

HUNDREDS OF PEOPLE DIED AS A RESULT OF HURRICANE KATRINA, THOUGH NO ONE KNOWS FOR SURE HOW MANY PEOPLE LOST THEIR LIVES IN THE MASSIVE STORM AND THE FLOODING THAT FOLLOWED.

TAMING NATURE

Water is always moving somewhere—from rivers and lakes to streams and oceans. These waterways provide food for people and animals and water for plants to grow, and help people move from place to place.

Natural sources of water usually follow a path carved into the earth. But getting lots of rain can make a waterway flood. This can cause damage to everything around it. Crops and plants can get flooded, and buildings can be destroyed by the damage. Levees and seawalls are built to stop water from moving into places where it could harm human life.

PEOPLE OFTEN BUILD CITIES WHERE THE MOUTH OF A RIVER MEETS A LARGER BODY OF WATER SUCH AS AN OCEAN. WHEN WATERS RISE, HOWEVER, THE CITIES THEN NEED PROTECTION FROM FLOODING.

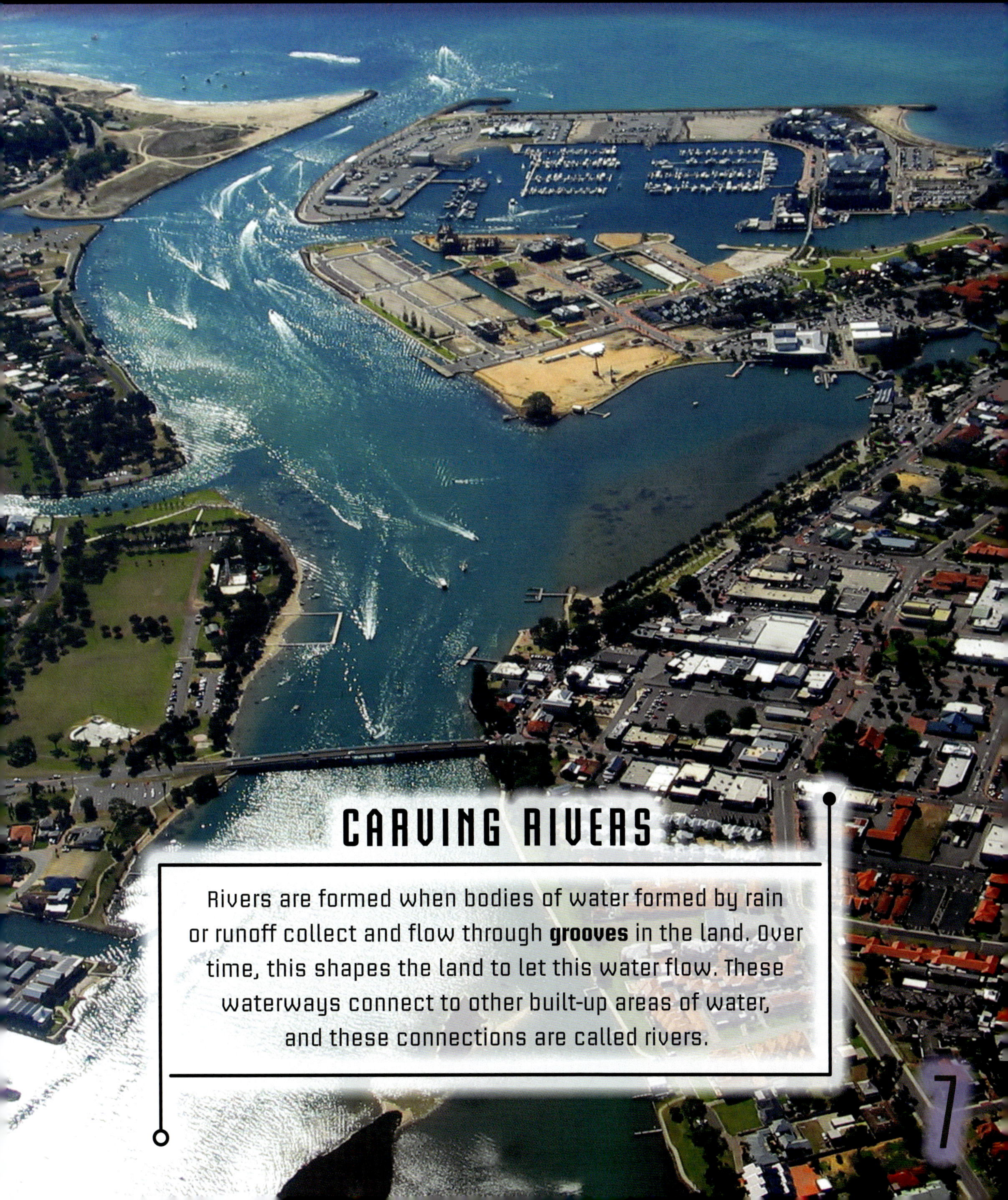

CARVING RIVERS

Rivers are formed when bodies of water formed by rain or runoff collect and flow through **grooves** in the land. Over time, this shapes the land to let this water flow. These waterways connect to other built-up areas of water, and these connections are called rivers.

DIRT PYRAMIDS

The first known levees were built in India around 2500 BC. The Harappan people of the Indus River valley used these levees to keep floodwaters out of their cities and away from their crops.

A common way to make a levee is to pile up earth on a flat surface. Levees are wider at the bottom and narrower at the top. If you cut through a levee and look at the cut end, it resembles a pyramid with a flat top instead of a pointed one. Plants such as grass are often grown atop levees so water doesn't wash the earth away.

DIRT LEVEE ALONG SAN FRANCISCO BAY

THE PLANTS GROWN ATOP DIRT LEVEES HOLD THE EARTH TOGETHER TO HELP STOP **EROSION**.

LEVEES IN ANCIENT EGYPT

Early Egyptians built their own levees starting about 3,000 years ago. Over a long period of time, they constructed many levees along the Nile River, the longest river in the world. This series of levees stretched for over 600 miles (966 km)!

DIFFERENT KINDS OF LEVEES

Not all levees are man-made. Natural levees are often made by floodwaters! Bits of matter called sediment are in floodwaters and often get left behind on land when the water level goes down. These natural levees are also created when rivers have many twists and turns. The sediment is left behind in these corners and the levee slowly grows larger.

The levees people make are called artificial levees. They're made by piling concrete, rocks, soil, or sand to form a wall. Sometimes sandbags are used at the top of levees to better hold them in place.

LEVEE TOPPED WITH SANDBAGS

WHEN LEVEES FAIL, LIKE THIS ONE ALONG THE SACRAMENTO RIVER IN CALIFORNIA, THEY MUST BE REPAIRED AND MADE STRONGER.

DANGEROUS LEVEES

Levees can be hard to maintain in dangerous areas. California's levee system, for example, is considered dangerous because of **earthquakes**. These natural events can shake the ground and break levees. California has **invested** over $700 million in its levee system since 1973, but more money is needed to make the system safer.

PREVENTING FAILURE

Levees need to be **monitored** to make sure they're working properly. The Army Corps of Engineers says that levees near cities need to be built high enough to handle a 10-year flood, or a flood that has a 10 percent chance of happening in a year. Levees are also watched closely for signs of erosion and other drainage problems.

Inspectors look for cracks in levees or even unwanted plants or animals nearby. Animals can make holes in the levee by burrowing, or digging, which can cause leaks. Sandbags or other **temporary** measures can be added to levees to make them stronger in case of **emergencies**.

NEW ORLEANS HOPES TO IMPROVE ITS LEVEES SO THEY COULD STAND UP TO A 500-YEAR STORM, OR ONE THAT HAS A 0.2 PERCENT CHANCE OF HAPPENING EVERY YEAR.

COUNTING THE YEARS

Engineers working to build levees measure their readiness using years. A 100-year storm, for example, is a storm so strong it's only expected to happen once every 100 years. That storm, though, would have a 1 percent chance of happening every year. Hurricane Katrina was considered a 150-year to 200-year storm in New Orleans.

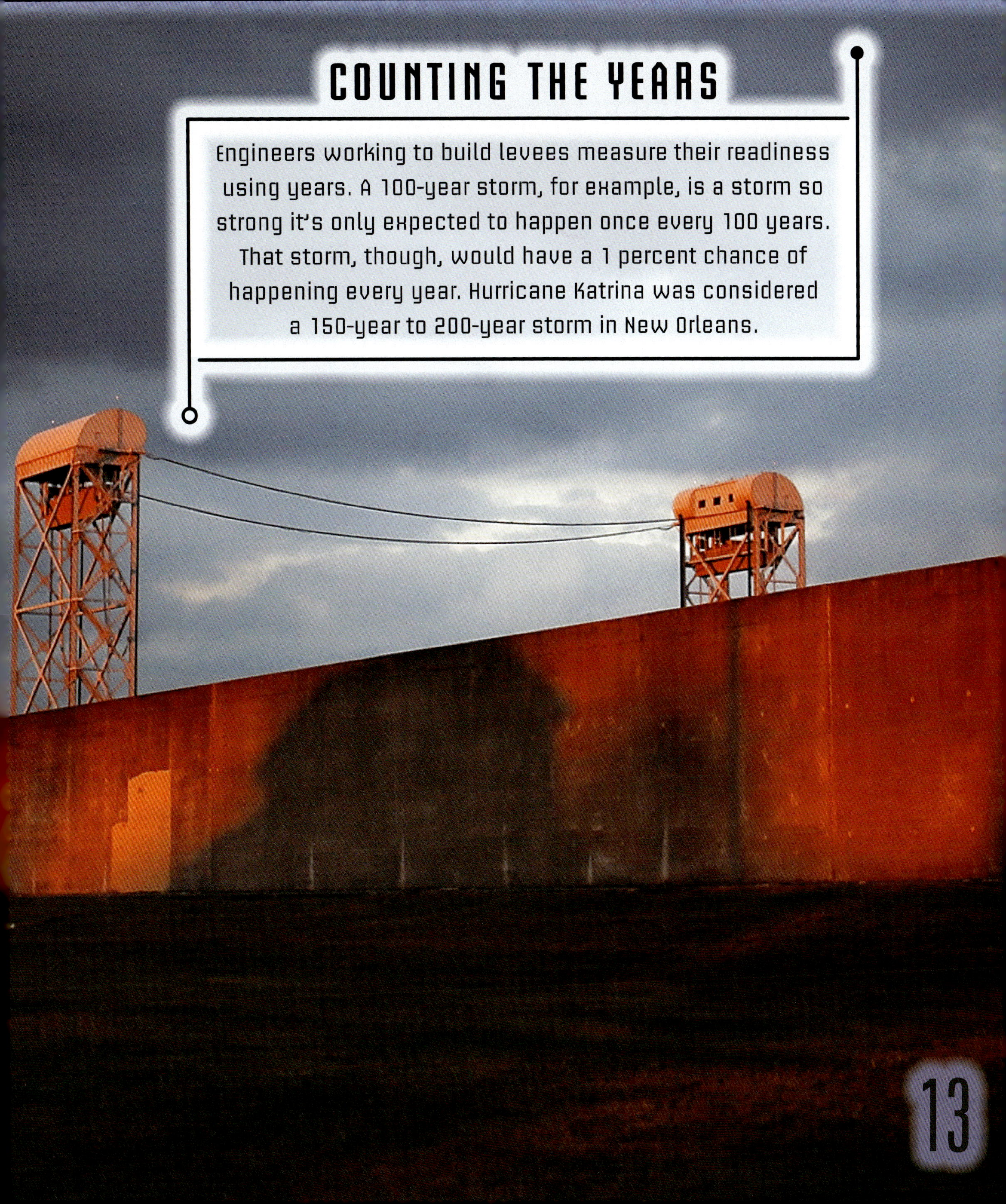

WHEN LEVEES FAIL

Levees fail when they can no longer hold back the weight of the water. But how they fail can happen a few different ways. The first is that the weight and force of the water pushes through a weak section of a levee.

A second kind of failure happens when a river's water level rises too high and water flows over a levee. This is called overtopping.

A third way is that a levee becomes **saturated** with water. When this happens, the levee itself is worn away, and water is let through to the other side, causing a failure.

WHEN A LEVEE FAILURE HAS BEEN CAUSED BY WATER SEEPING UNDER THE LEVEE, IT'S CALLED CREVASSE. "CREVASSE" IS ANOTHER NAME FOR A LARGE CRACK.

LEVEES RAISE WATER?

When levees are built, they can often raise the water level of the body they're trying to hold back. This is because a levee can trap the sediment in the river, letting it build up on the riverbed. Between 1850 and 1927, the levees built to control the Mississippi River were continuously raised to battle the riverbed's rise.

BUILDING AGAIN

When levees fail, they must be fixed. Fortunately, levees that are broken can still be rebuilt without having to start all over again. Often floods will only break through weak parts of a levee, leaving the rest of the structure in place. When rebuilding levees, it's easier to make them better because engineers will know what went wrong before.

After Hurricane Katrina, New Orleans's levees were rebuilt to better protect the city from floodwaters. Engineers made them stronger and also created structures called surge barriers, which act like gates that keep water out in case the levees break again.

HURRICANE KATRINA RECOVERY

Rebuilding after Katrina was very hard. Because the city lies below sea level and has water on all sides, it had to be pumped out because floodwaters had nowhere to drain. Parts of the city were cut off from rescue teams, and flooding made travel very hard. It took many years to fix the levees and rebuild homes lost in the flooding.

NEW ORLEANS IS A CITY BUILT BETWEEN WATER, WITH THE GULF OF MEXICO, THE MISSISSIPPI RIVER, LAKE BORGNE, AND LAKE PONTCHARTRAIN SURROUNDING IT ON ALL SIDES.

REBUILDING A LEVEE AFTER HURRICANE KATRINA

BATTLING THE OCEANS

Levees are important for controlling rivers that cut through the land, but what about water from the ocean? Oceans can swell from storms and rising tide, which can lead to serious flooding. Towns and cities that are near the coastline are at risk of being overtaken by nature's largest bodies of water.

Sometimes sea levels can rise so much that the sea can **encroach** and swallow parts of the land. Often this movement can put open land underwater for good. To stop the advance of the ocean onto the land, people build seawalls.

OCEAN WAVES ARE FORMED BY A NUMBER OF DIFFERENT FACTORS, AND THEIR HEIGHT CAN BE HARD TO HOLD BACK WHEN STORMS OR HURRICANES MAKE LANDFALL.

OCEAN FACTS

More than 70 percent of Earth's surface is completely covered in water. That's about 140 million square miles (363 million sq km) of land covered by water. Earth's oceans are 2.3 miles (3.7 km) deep on average, with the deepest point being almost 7 miles (11 km) deep. And humans have explored less than 10 percent of our oceans!

TYPES OF SEAWALLS

There are three main kinds of seawall. The first is called a vertical seawall. Vertical seawalls are high, flat walls and are meant to face high-energy waves. These seawalls are best for places that have a lot of large waves hitting the same spot very often. They also help protect the shoreline from erosion.

The second kind of seawall is called a curved seawall. Curved seawalls bend to follow the shape of the shoreline. The wall's curve helps disperse, or spread out, some of the wave energy. Unlike the stiff vertical walls, these can be made to fit their surroundings, but often cost more.

CURVED SEAWALL

THE GALVESTON SEAWALL WAS BUILT AFTER A BAD HURRICANE KILLED MANY PEOPLE IN GALVESTON, TEXAS, IN 1900.

SEAWALL ART

The Galveston Seawall in Galveston, Texas, is a vertical seawall that's 10 miles (16 km) long and 17 feet (5.2 m) high. It's famous for showing the world's longest and largest mural, or wall art. Planned by Peter Davis, the mural is 2.4 miles (3.9 km) long. It features pictures of birds, sea life, and famous sights from the city.

A third kind of seawall is called a mound seawall. Mound seawalls are usually not built to last a long time, but are made during emergencies when large storms are coming. Mound seawalls can be made from sandbags, bricks, rocks, or dirt. Some mound seawalls can be made permanent, or built to last a long time, after an emergency passes.

Mound seawalls are good for stopping smaller, lower-energy waves. They're cheaper to make than other seawalls, but don't last as long. They may have to be continually rebuilt after even small storms.

PILE IT ON!

Sandbags are often used to make mound seawalls because they're cheap and easy to use. They're often lined up along beaches, but can sometimes be put in front of buildings for extra protection. Strangely enough, the beach is being protected from the ocean by sand, something that it's made of!

MOUND SEAWALL

SOME SHORELINES, LIKE THIS ONE IN AGUA VISTA PARK IN SAN FRANCISCO, USE ROCK CALLED RIP-RAP TO PROTECT THEIR SOIL FROM EROSION.

PLANTS AND ANIMALS

Seawalls protect human habitats, or homes, but they may change other organisms' homes. Algae and plants can have a hard time growing in front of seawalls. Tall walls stopping water from flowing may keep fish from moving upstream and harm plant life as well.

Because of this, some seawalls are built to actually help plants grow. A new seawall in Seattle, Washington, for example, was shaped with rounded areas where algae can grow. Animals such as starfish and mussels can use these studs to grab hold and live, too. Bags of stones have also been added at the bottom to help fish like salmon find food and hide.

CLIMATE CHANGE

Climate change, or the gradual changing of Earth's climate patterns due in part to human activity, will make seawalls more important in the future. As ocean levels rise and large storms happen more often, seawalls will need to save oceanfront homes and land from being retaken by the waves.

CITIES SUCH AS MIAMI, NEW ORLEANS, AND NEW YORK CITY WILL NEED MORE SEAWALLS TO PROTECT PEOPLE AND BUILDINGS AS CLIMATE CHANGE AFFECTS SEA LEVELS.

CHANGING THE BEACHES

Seawalls can save buildings and towns from ocean waves, but sometimes they can harm the beaches they're built on. If a beach is already eroding, seawalls can speed up that process by causing passive erosion. This is when water in front of the wall starts to deepen, causing the shoreline to be pushed back into the wall and washing away the beach in front of it.

Sometimes seawalls can cause active erosion, where they cause beaches to lose sand because of the way the wall causes waves to behave. A wall built in the wrong place can often make the beach lose sand faster.

SURF'S NOT UP

Seawalls can sometimes cause shallow areas of a beach to deepen. Shallow areas are needed to create breaking waves, which are the kinds of waves surfers use to ride across the water. Without shallow areas near the beach, surfing areas can potentially be ruined for beachgoers.

STORMS CAN CAUSE THE MAKEUP AND SHAPE OF BEACHES TO CHANGE QUICKLY. EVEN STURDY AREAS CAN QUICKLY BE WASHED AWAY BY STRONG WAVES.

FUTURE WAVES

Some people think levees and seawalls will be made with different material in the future. Geotextiles are **fabrics** that can be used with soil to help reinforce water barriers. These can filter the water and let it in, but still protect against a wave's energy. They're often used in mound seawalls to help fight erosion of the beach.

Others think engineers will find better ways to use concrete and sandbags to protect us in the future. Better monitoring and study of how these structures work against water will help them last longer. As long as water flows, people will try to change its course.

GEOTEXTILES

FIGHTING FLOODS

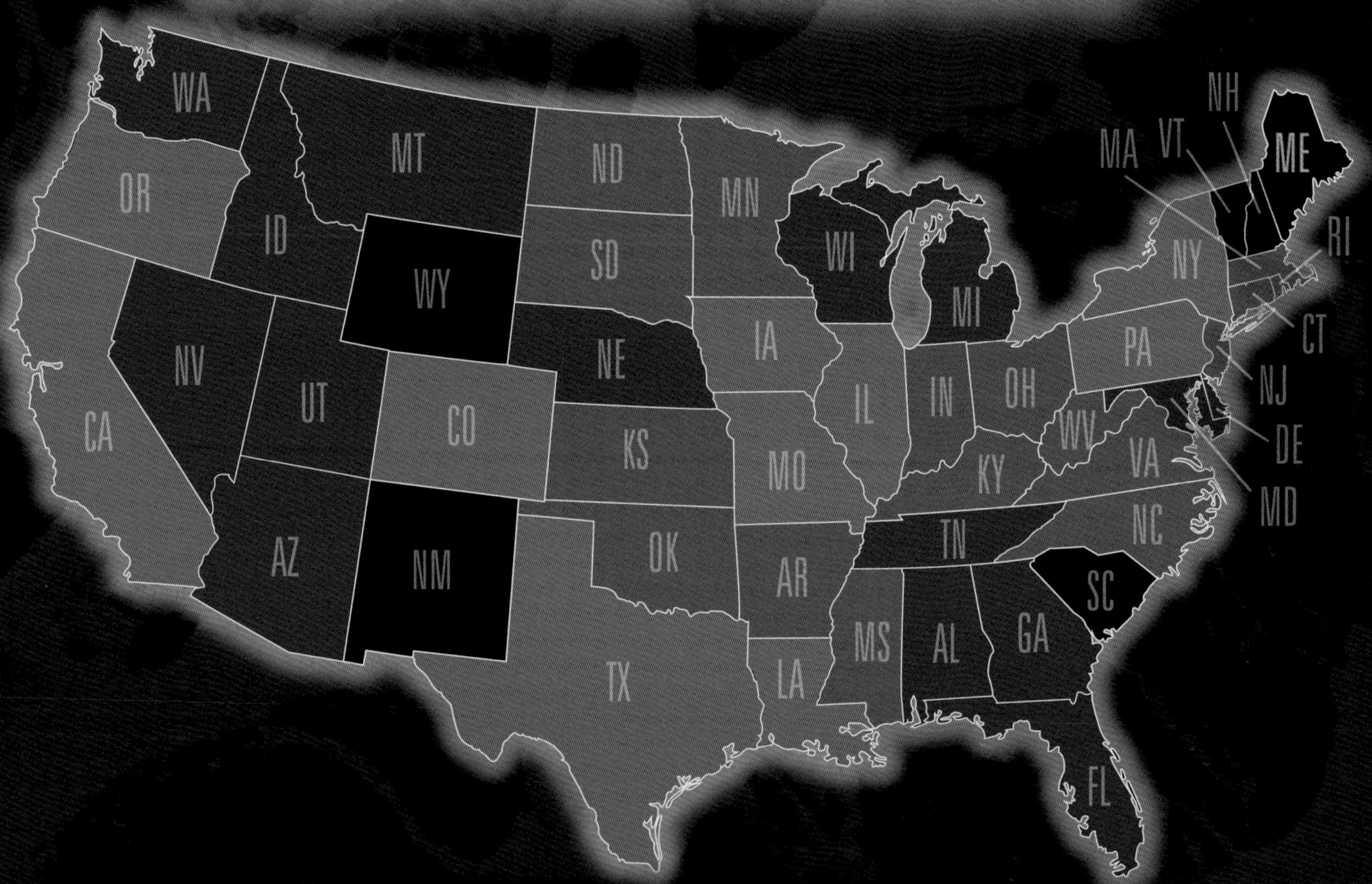

AVERAGE SPENT PER YEAR ON FLOOD DAMAGE

$.47 MILLION–$18.8 MILLION

$27.3 MILLION–$65.06 MILLION

$85.73 MILLION–$156.8 MILLION

$197.8 MILLION–$682.3 MILLION

THE COSTS OF WATER PROTECTION

Between 2010 and 2015, the United States saw $34 billion in damage from major floods. These numbers are huge compared to the cost of building a levee. In New Orleans, for example, rebuilding levees cost around $14 billion, while the storm itself caused $96 billion in damage. While levees are expensive, they're definitely worth the investment!

GLOSSARY

damage: loss or harm done to a person or place

earthquake: a shaking of the ground caused by the movement of Earth's crust

emergency: an unexpected situation that needs quick action

encroach: to advance beyond the usual limits

erosion: the act of wearing away by water, wind, or ice

fabric: cloth

groove: a long, narrow space worn into a surface

invest: to put money into something to gain a benefit

levee: a wall built to keep river and lake water out of a certain place

monitor: to watch closely

saturate: to completely fill, as with a liquid, so that it cannot take in any more

seawall: a wall built to stop ocean waves from reaching a certain place

temporary: lasting for a short time

FOR MORE INFORMATION

BOOKS

Mattern, Joanne. *Floods, Dams, and Levees.* Vero Beach, FL: Rourke Publishing, 2012.

Stefoff, Rebecca. *Building Dikes and Levees.* New York, NY: Cavendish Square, 2016.

WEBSITES

Levee
nationalgeographic.org/encyclopedia/levee/
Find more information about levees and see pictures of them here.

Rebuilding the Levees
sciencechannel.com/tv-shows/build-it-bigger/videos/build-it-bigger-rebuilding-the-levees/
Watch a video about rebuilding levees after Hurricane Katrina here.

Publisher's note to educators and parents: Our editors have carefully reviewed these websites to ensure that they are suitable for students. Many websites change frequently, however, and we cannot guarantee that a site's future contents will continue to meet our high standards of quality and educational value. Be advised that students should be closely supervised whenever they access the Internet.

INDEX